The Dawning

An Awakening Unto Her Own Worth

A collection of poems celebrating
Our resilience as we walk through
The darkness towards the new light!
A new hope!

By Eleanor Sybil D'Cruz

Chennai • Bangalore

CLEVER FOX PUBLISHING
Chennai, India

Published by CLEVER FOX PUBLISHING 2024
Copyright © Eleanor Sybil D'Cruz 2024

All Rights Reserved.
ISBN: 978-93-56487-54-3

This book has been published with all reasonable efforts taken to make the material error-free after the consent of the author. No part of this book shall be used, reproduced in any manner whatsoever without written permission from the author, except in the case of brief quotations embodied in critical articles and reviews.

The Author of this book is solely responsible and liable for its content including but not limited to the views, representations, descriptions, statements, information, opinions and references ["Content"]. The Content of this book shall not constitute or be construed or deemed to reflect the opinion or expression of the Publisher or Editor. Neither the Publisher nor Editor endorse or approve the Content of this book or guarantee the reliability, accuracy or completeness of the Content published herein and do not make any representations or warranties of any kind, express or implied, including but not limited to the implied warranties of merchantability, fitness for a particular purpose. The Publisher and Editor shall not be liable whatsoever for any errors, omissions, whether such errors or omissions result from negligence, accident, or any other cause or claims for loss or damages of any kind, including without limitation, indirect or consequential loss or damage arising out of use, inability to use, or about the reliability, accuracy or sufficiency of the information contained in this book.

Dedication

I dedicate this book to my daughter

Grace Sanah Sherring.

She is my heartbeat.

My reason.

****

Foreword

Eleanor is my elder (by 6 full months) cousin/sister. We have been each other's support system for our entire lives. She is also my favourite jiving partner.

Eleanor has opened her heart and soul in this book. It's a book that has unashamedly dealt with our pain and loss. I'm sure that many of us will be able to relate to the pain embedded in the poems here and the strength to overcome them.

Eleanor has always loved reading and writing. She would hide under the quilt and read murder mysteries all night.
She has been through many phases. There was a time when she was sure she would be an artist so she splattered paint all over the place. She was yelled at by our grandmother innumerable times because she would climb up ladders as she wanted to help the workers paint the house too. Thank goodness she outgrew that phase. Then there was the carpentry phase where the veranda was littered with sandpaper, nails and spilt varnish. Thank goodness she outgrew that too.

The two phases that have stuck are baking and writing… and I hope she never outgrows either of these two phases.
When Ele asked me to write this foreword she was looking for someone who has been with her in most of these trials, someone who has too been entwined in pain.

These poems are mirrors of our lives, not just mine as I am family but also about the lives of us women in general.

I hope this book reaches the maximum number of women to resonate with them and let them know that they aren't alone.

Laurena Moore Simlai

****

Acknowledgement

This book has only been made possible because I was taught by the best.

I thank my parents Mr. Bernard D'Cruz and Mrs. Audrey D'Cruz née Moore for the hours of teaching and training that they undertook to instil in me the art of writing. I thank my uncle and aunt Mr. Francis W Moore and Mrs Caroline Moore née Cottee for their love and support. A special thank you to my dear aunt Mrs. Patience Guzder who was my moral support. She would make me as comfortable as possible, with a bowl of steaming hot soup whenever I'd study at her quaint home.

I can't thank my dear cousin and best friend, Mrs. Laurena Moore Simali, enough for writing the foreword for this book. We have always been as thick as thieves and I'm blessed to have her in my life.

I'm heavily indebted to Mr. Shubhojoy Mitra for all the work he has put in, despite his hectic work schedule, to create this book cover.

I also thank my lovely friend, colleague and work daughter Ms Ambika Solanki for helping to lay out this book.

For all the times that I had my nose buried in notebooks and registers while oblivious to the world around me, I would like to thank Mr. Sooraj Sherring and Ms. Grace Sanah Sherring for all the support they have given me.

They say cousins are your first best friends and this is exactly who mine are. I thank them for always being my support system, for without their continuous prayers and support, I would probably not have made it thus far.

I would also like to thank each and every teacher of mine at St. Mary's Convent, Allahabad for all they taught me and for all the patience they showered on me throughout my schooling years.
Finally, I would like to thank all my friends, colleagues and students who have supported me in this endeavour.

****

Preface

A collection of poems based on the author's life experiences, dreams, desires and disappointments but through it, all the awakening of one's true self.

Her book is to help encourage women of all backgrounds, ages and cultures to rise like the Phoenix that they are and walk with their heads held high…No matter what the circumstance!

Women for centuries have been tortured by the ones closest to them, betrayed by the ones they have trusted the most and even murdered by the ones for whom they would have gladly given their own lives. They have been deceived and lied to, sometimes for years together!

The amazing thing about women is that even though they may not know … they Know!!!

They sometimes choose to play the 'fool', ignore the red flags, look the other way, and pretend to be deaf, dumb and blind only because they prioritise family, home and others before themselves. Their strength lies in the fact that their hearts rule their heads and therefore to take their kindness for weakness is the singular biggest mistake that anyone can make, solely because in reality, the biggest loser is the deceiver himself!

Women! You have to learn to prioritise yourself, only because no one else is going to do that for you!

****

Content

1. My Haven (Introduction)
2. Daddy
3. Those Red Bricks
4. Somehow
5. Scars
6. Retrace
7. Disfigure
8. The Leash - Unleashed
9. The Other Woman
10. Team Not Mine
11. Appreciate
12. Walk Away
13. School Friends
14. Give Wings To Your Dreams
15. Sundays
16. Trees
17. A Year
18. Hands
19. A Chasm Afar (To Arpit, you will always be loved. With love from Mom)
20. Forever In Your Corner
21. Arise Oh humanity! Arise!
22. Hate
23. What's Your Threshold?
24. Handsome
25. His Lies
26. Pride
27. Simple Things
28. Our Journeys
29. Time

30. Money
31. Hospital Truths
32. The Spiritual Camouflage
33. Resuscitate Your Dying Soul
34. Life's Race
35. I'm Sorry
36. Be Your Own Break Of Day!
37. Me
38. Imagination
39. Just Be The Friend She'd Call
40. The Dawning

1. <u>My Haven</u> **(Introduction)**

Whom do I tell?

And what do I say?

Life's hurts - These gulps of gall.

For whom do I trust?

And who has the time to listen in?

And why should they anyway?

It's therefore best

I free my soul

And let my pen

Bleed for me...

To set my heart

For some time, free…

My pen

My paper

My thoughts

For me.

To pen a little haven

A haven unto my own!

A place where stones bear wings

And coloured crows sing

A place of love eternal

Where pain has no place

And tears are unknown

My utopian dream realised

Realised in ...

My pen

My paper

My haven....
****

2. **Daddy**

{Losing a parent at any age is devastating. Losing my daddy at the age of ten was the first curveball life threw at me. It most probably turned the course of my thinking and forced me to grow up faster than I normally would have.}

Daddy! Daddy! Daddy!

A word so faint yet sweet,

I never thought a word so quaint,

Would on my lips, ever now meet!

Tender hands and arms so strong,

Could now never me enfold,

Though many a tear my eye did bear,

The Lord God I did hold.

Heavenly arms of mercy sweet,

Hold me close like never before,

And hands which wipe away each tear,

Are gentle to the core!

Thank you, Lord, my saviour sweet,

Thou knew each pain and fear,

And delivered me from them all,

And called me daughter dear!

****

3. Those Red Bricks

{There is a certain unforgettable familiarity with even the most insignificant of objects in the house that one grows up in. Life in its unpredictability can sometimes cause miles to come between you and the life that you once knew, causing even the most mundane objects to suddenly become little beacons of nostalgia.}

I know each brick

And they recognise me

I know each brick

And they know me.

They know me better

Than those who should

They understand me more

My very core.

They've borne my first steps

Toddling walking skipping running

They've seen each time
I got up after a fall.

They've watched my blood dry

From each cut and scrape.

They've witnessed those tears

In those long lonely walks.

They've seen me learn to cycle

And my dad who taught me to

They've seen me walk

Behind his coffin too.

They've seen me happy

Sad and angry

My teenage tantrums

My fancy NCC uniform

My waiting for a crush

My ecstasy over my first salary

My wedding ceremony

And my longing to return.

They've seen me walk away

They've seen me leave

But will I ever see them again?

Just once again

Will I walk on them once more?

Just once more

Those bricks

Those simple red bricks.

****

4. **Somehow**

{There are times when hurts and misconceptions caused by 'misplaced baggage' can cause unintended rifts in even the most pious relationships for no sensible reason. These can embitter one's life forever and take a turn for the worst, thus robbing families of a lifetime of memorable moments. Taking away the chance of celebrating precious old memories and creating precious new ones. Taking away the chance of healing together… forever.}

Today the phone didn't ring…

And neither did I dial.

Today I never longed to hear her voice …

And I'm sure she did neither!

At least the fake love has faded

At least I no longer pretend

An appearance of what is right

When my soul can no longer win!

I haven't heard my lips whisper

It's alien even to type

The name that once was always

On the tip of my tongue.

That name

That word

It's hard to believe

Is now so far-flung

From my heart 'n from my mind

But then

It somehow lingers on

Somehow…

Somehow.

****

5. <u>Scars</u>

{Throughout her life a woman is made to feel inadequate because of her scars. Be they the scars across her face, the scars left from a C-Section or even the stretch marks left... after literally creating a new life on the planet... they are seen as imperfections!

Those that should be a normal part of life are seen as something that should be covered up either with some fancy vanishing cream or surgery... Why? For what reason? We are human and it's perfectly normal to have scars.

And then there are those emotional wounds... which have caused those unseen scars. Those which we hide with a smile or mask with humour or even camouflage with aggression.

Both ... Physically and ... Emotionally ... as long as they are now just scars and not still raw open wounds. For, if they are still wounds, that still hurt, that still bleed, that are filled with pus causing excruciating pain... then it is high time you start working towards healing them... and changing those raw open festering wounds into the victorious symbols of an overcomer! Embrace your scars!}

Each scar tells a story,

Each scar tells a tale,

An insight into history,

A glimpse into the pain!

It tells of a survivor,

Of one who overcame,

Of one who has been through,

The fire and the flame!

It's the witness of the healing,

Of the will to carry on,

To build a new tomorrow,

To build a brand new dawn!

****

6. **Retrace**

{Sometimes in life we are forced to look at the bigger picture. Is it prescriptive? No, not at all. This depends on the situation. It depends on you! It is not always conducive and certainly not always safe. If one had to do it all over again ...would one? No, not necessarily. Perspectives change!}

At the shutting of the door,

To the life, I want no more.

At the tossing of the key,

To the chance of breaking free.

I see my baby standing by,

Torn and shattered in her cry.

All my steps I will retrace,

To bring that smile upon her face.

And in the sunshine of that smile,

I will walk the extra mile.

****

7. <u>Disfigure</u>

{One early morning my helper walked in with bruises all over her. Her husband in a drunken state had decided that she wasn't worthy of the respect she deserved. She had refused to give him her hard-earned money to fulfil his drinking addiction. What gave him the right to raise his hand on her? The idea that marriage is an ever-lasting utopia is hogwash if respect and equality are absent.}

Your face isn't meant to be slapped!

And your hair isn't meant to be yanked!

Your eye isn't meant to be blacked!

And your back isn't meant to be kicked!

If you think you're keeping the peace

By hiding your pain,

If you think you're saving your marriage

You're trying in vain,

Coz the covenant was broken

Long before he lifted his finger,

It broke when he thought

You were his toy to disfigure!
****

8. The Leash

{The invisible social leash put on women has caused many of our mothers and grandmothers to live lives of untold curtailment, forcing them to sacrifice an innumerable number of their dreams and ambitions at the hands of an extremely overbearing and toxic society. Is this attitude now completely in the past? One would wish... but alas it isn't.}

She'll bring a stain upon our name,

So put her on a leash!

Her victimhood will bring us shame,

So keep her on a leash!

It may be someone else's crime,

But keep her on the leash!

She may try to heal with time,

Just tighten that leash!

How dare she try to speak so fine,

Add a muzzle to the leash!

And if to fly she shows incline,

Just strengthen that leash!

She's a woman, she's a girl, she's a she!

Therefore, a leash it must certainly be!

For on the leash, she must stay,

With little scope to swing or sway!

For if unbridled she may dream,

And will then act to realise her dream!

And woe betide us if her act,

Brings shame upon our social pact!

For whether she be at fault or not,

The shame and stigma will be brought!

Thus nip this flower in the bud,

Let her grovel in the mud!

For if she flies,

She'll expose our lies!

Thus on the leash, she must stay,

With little hope to swing and sway!

Unleashed

Oh! Your leash is full of lies,

Myths and fears behind its lies!

Your insecurities she will expose,

And your leash she will dispose!

For if she has the strength to cry,

She has the strength to wipe them dry!

And with the very dust in which she lay,

She'll use that dust to pave her way!

For rise, she will and rise she must,

As that leash begins to rust!

Her walk, her run, her flight, and more,

Like an eagle, she will soar!

For she's a Woman, she's a Girl, she's a She!

Therefore, triumphant she will certainly be!

****

9. The Other Woman

{Extramarital affairs weigh heavily upon the well-being of the entire family and are the cause of a lot of pain and heartache. The people involved are said to be selfish and most probably rightly so. But shouldn't they share the blame equally? Aren't they 50-50 partners in crime? Yet, somehow society finds ways to blame the 'other woman' for her crime while her partner gets away with being reprimanded for a misdemeanour.

While the root cause may be many, one root cause is definitely the lack of self-value, of not knowing one's own worth. This poem is not to abide by the judgements of what a fickle society has to say or to follow the norms of a so-called honourable life but a message to all the ladies who have found themselves tied up in strings they never bargained for. It's a wakeup call to set themselves free and look for their purpose in life, to find their true worth.}

'The Other Woman'

Isn't the title that you deserve

Coz you are worth so much more

Than he can ever serve.

So treat yourself lavishly

To self-respect and dignity

And turn around and walk away

From this self-inflicted indignity.

Don't believe the lies he spins

And make his wife your enemy,

For, you'll find his yarns spin thin

And a very different reality.

Understand your own true worth

That you should be an eternal treasure

And not one to be used and discarded

After a selfish momentary pleasure.

No matter how he cries and moans

Know the direction in which he'll swing

That he's only out for fleeting fun

And he honours not the golden ring.

For, if he finds this his thrill

To cheat on her with you,

He will seek this very thrill

To cheat on you too.

Age and time will deter him not

He'll cheat and cheat again

Not realising his wrinkles

Could hold Cherrapunji's rain.

So turn your back on him today

Sashay 'n sway as you walk away

On him don't waste another day

Find your true worth, I pray.

****

10. Team - Not Mine

{Betrayal. The sinking feeling of suddenly being completely thrust aside by them whom you considered your very own, could send anyone to the brink of deep despair. On the calming of the mind, you will realise that they never were on your team.

You will realise that you have continuously ignored all the red flags that kept fluttering in the background. It is then that you must take a stand for yourself, knowing that in reality, you've always really been alone. That team that you thought you had, was non-existent. They were with you physically because it suited them. You were a convenience and once your use to them had ended, you could be discarded within seconds. Additionally, you could also be absurdly blamed to justify their callous actions.

But take heart, for now you know where you stand. You can finally get your feet off the eggshells and onto solid ground. You could actually go a step further and build your own platform as you now don't have to toe the line or play the part.

Remember the upside of betrayal is ... Freedom.}

I thought we were one team,

How did I end up on the other side?

I thought we were one team,

But you've made an opponent of me.

I don't understand your politics,

I don't know how to play your games.

I don't understand your goals,

For you keep changing the rules.

I just want to walk away,

It's too confusing to stay.

I thought we were on the same team,

But it was obviously just a dream!

****

11. Appreciate (Qadr)

{Taken For Granted! When one has worked hard, all one needs is a little appreciation. Be this at home or the workplace, a token of appreciation or even a simple smile goes a long way.

To undervalue someone's existence in your life only causes one to retreat into a shell, in order to safeguard one's feelings. To cultivate a shell and thicken it takes time. Therefore, the thicker the shell, the deeper the feelings of being undervalued.

Thus setting off a chain of events with actions and reactions flying back and forth, the start of a vicious circle of Non Appreciation.}

Don't ask me why I'm not the same.

Don't ask me why I seem to have changed.

Don't ask me why I've distanced myself.

Don't ask me why I reflect what you portrayed.

Don't ask.

Don't you dare ask.

For deep down you know the truth.

For deep down you know you know the truth.

It's only now

That you know the feeling.

Just because

I've begun my own healing.
****

12. Walk Away

{Protecting yourself, to anchor yourself takes courage! Manifest it!}

You say

I've thrown you out

But

You walked out of the gate

I only bolted it

And now you knock

Kick and scream

And say

You want to come back in

Why?

Why!

Your shoes

Are still dirty

Covered in even more dust

Even more than before.

I've cleaned up the house

I've swabbed the floors

There are flowers in the vases

And there is perfume everywhere

It took time

And work

And

And it's beautiful

Now

It's beautiful now.

So

If I unbolt that gate

You'll bring in all that

Dust

Dirt

With you

Again

No no

No.

I can't do it all over again

I won't!

So leave

Just walk away.

Walk away.
****

13. School Friends

{Dedicated to all SMCites! St. Mary's Convent Allahabad you Rock!}

We ate from each other's tiffins,

We copied each other's homework,

Got punished together for giggling,

At some silly secret joke.

I rushed to pick you up when you fell,

And knew you'd do the same for me,

Coz you and I were one team,

'You and I' were We!

Our tear-stained faces at our farewell,

Summoned an era goodbye,

And in that last and final huddle,

There wasn't a single dry eye.

As life took its course,

I wondered where you might be,

And all our crazy escapades,

Became my daughter's bedtime stories.

And when on social media,

I suddenly saw your name,

My joy knew no boundaries,

I had found my friend again.

And as we chatted, giggled, and gossiped,

We were back in the classroom and school hall,

My sister, my friend, my prank partner,

Was back in my life after all.

Now I stand by you in life's turmoil,

And know you do the same for me,

Coz you and I are still one team,

'You and I' are 'We'!

****

14. Give Wings To Your Dreams!

{To anyone who has given up on your dreams- Don't!}

If you think your dreams

Have lost their wings,

Just take a deep breath and recall,

Your bright-eyed self,

Who believed she could win,

No matter how hard the fall!

For, she dusted herself

To resume her game,

And once in the game,

She forgot her pain,

With cuts, scrapes on a scabby knee,

Ran right into the midst of it all.

For her eyes shone bright,

And nothing could deter her glee.

So, now close your eyes,

And search within,

That bright-eyed girl

Who's hidden within,

Awaits a signal from you

For no cuts or scrapes of a scabby life

Can deter her will

Or dim that light in her eye!

So get up girl

And dust yourself

Resume your game,

Believe you can win,

To give wings to your dreams,

And make them fly anew!

****

15. **Sundays**

{The joy of growing up in good ole Allahabad in the 80s and 90s.}

It was a quiet pleasant Sunday

When I met this charming fellow

He looked so neat and pristine

With a voice so deep and mellow.

Now he had just bought a new bike

And it obviously filled him with pride

When suddenly in a voice so deep

He offered to teach me to ride.

Hesitant I was but he argued

It'd be good to learn something new

But as we began I realised

He hadn't thought it through.

For the words he began chanting were alien
Which, apparently he thought I knew
Gear, brake, clutch he screamed
And I think he was turning blue.

Now his voice had suddenly turned squeaky
And so terribly terribly shrill
That I had to turn around to check
If it was his mother or him still!

Lookout, watch out, go straight he screeched
In an octave of the highest pitch
And apparently, his fears weren't unfounded
For the road had made a geographical switch.

Now I thought I was riding on the road
With the Bishop's garden beside me
And beside me, it should have remained
Instead, it loomed right in front of me.

Now because I was young and agile

And survival mode had kicked in

With some simple acrobatics

I jumped off to save my skin.

I thought that screeching soul behind me

Would have done the very same

Instead, I saw him half lying on the seat

Grappling with the handle in vain.

And as he rampaged through the garden

Beheading roses with horsepower might

His skidding and somersaulting in the mud

Was an extremely unpleasant sight.

Then kind folk came running

To sympathise and help poor me

Of course, some even rushed to help

The one lying crumpled under a tree.

And as he was helped to stand

Gingerly upon his feet

I noticed a frown and an angry glare

Where his muddy brows did meet.

Now it's been 25 years and still counting

And he still hasn't spoken to me

But I heard he's recently bought a new car

And I wonder if his Sundays are free!

****

16. Trees

{Deforestation- The bane of the planet.}

All those afternoons that I spent
Enjoying the summer breeze
Cradled in your lofty branches
In a world surrounded by trees.

I'm sorry I took you for granted
I never knew we'd lose
The joys of playing around you
To the corporate greedy noose.

With surgical precision, they've axed you
And changed our horizon forever
From the vibrant shades of green
To an avaricious concrete quagmire.

But all's not lost and there's still hope

For in hope for you, there's hope for me

For my very survival depends on you

And not on some covetous company.

And just like once you cradled me

I must do the same for you

And plant a tree wherever I go

And watch the horizon get back its hue.

****

17. <u>A Year!</u>

{Dedicated to my best friend Leona aka Minnie and my brother-in-law Dale. I wrote this a year after Covid-19 had raised its evil head and had snatched away so many of our loved ones. Life hasn't been the same without them. I miss them so much. Our little group just isn't the same anymore. We were all supposed to grow old together. Hide each other's walking sticks, steal each other's reading glasses and go on that long-awaited vacation together. But...}

In this year of trials still,

Living without you has been a battle uphill!

A year without your hearty laughter,

Jokes, advice and prayers!

We can't believe it's been a year,

We love 'n cherish your memories dear!

Our little group just isn't the same!

Without you, we are lost and lame!

I know it's just a curtain between us,

Life 'n death's translucent divide between us!

But we are broken!Oh! So Broken!

Our deeply loved family

Isn't what it used to be.

But hopefully, one joyful day,

If, we let not our faith go astray,

We shall someday,

Stay together,

Forever.

****

18. Hands

{It was during this time of darkness that we discovered our true friends... A heartfelt thank you to all who stepped up to step in.}

As life ebbs away from us,

Proving pain isn't a distant thing,

The hands that suddenly hold our own,

Prove love isn't distant too!

For though the hours be dark and bleak,

It illuminates those hands which hold our own,

For in that loss, we stand to gain,

A love that be steadfast through the pain!

And as those hands entwine with ours,

They shield and sheath our hearts with love,

For hands that come in love that way,

Already tested, will forever stay!

****

19. A Chasm Afar
To Arpit, With love from Mom: -

{To every sister who has suffered a miscarriage. You're not alone. You're still a mom because even though your arms may not hold your precious angel, your heart always will.

Hopefully, our little angels will meet us on some happy day.}

The moment I discovered that I cradled you

That I was to become your mummy

My whole world turned upside down

And everything looked brand new

The universe suddenly fell into place

And life seemed perfect,

As I floated on the pinnacle of maternal joy

I dreamt of how I'd raise my little boy

Of all the virtues that you'd imbibe

Being loving, kind and truthful

I dedicated you to Lord Jesus Christ

And named you, Arpit.

My feet hardly touched the floor

As I walked into the doctor's office

The clinic looked so adorable

Decked with pictures of babies

I avariciously read each poster

Of pre and postnatal care,

I entered her office with a smile

Expecting to see her smile too

Instead the worried look upon her face

And the concern in her voice

Heralded in a gush of fear

And a feeling of overwhelming despair.

The next few days were an open-eyed nightmare

Shuttling between clinics and pathology labs

And finally, when the reports were ready

The diagnosis made my heart sink

Termination was the verdict

For they felt my life was in danger.

As I struggled to comprehend what it meant

I promised to protect you as best as I could

That abortion wasn't an option for me

For you were my most precious blessing

And nothing was going to steal that away

We'd cherish whatever time we had together.

So wiping away those tell-tales signs of a sinking heart

Lost in a world of you and me

I read to you stories and parables

But didn't dare venture a tune

In case you'd copy me sing

I told you about your family

And what each one meant to me

Of all the fun you'd have with them

Hoping and praying you'd meet each one

I cradled you as best as I could

Just you 'n me in a cocoon of love

I'd whisper how much you mean to me.

The route to the hospital became all too familiar

With medicine piled upon the bedside table

When some visitors from the abortion advisory board

Said that the pain I was in, was too much for them.

What did they know of the joy you brought me!

That with each kick of yours, my heart did sing,

That when I'd talk to you, you'd be so calm

And the moment I'd stop you'd kick me again.

Oh! how I loved every movement of yours

How I yearned to capture it forevermore

"Just a few months more," I'd repeat to myself

While I yearned to hold you in a blanket and sing.

And just as I thought things were smooth

Loving each moment of expecting you

Collecting little clothes, blankets and toys,

I packed an emergency suitcase

Hoping against hope

It would only be to bring you back home,

Home, to me.

But on the night of the ninth

A nightmare jolted me awake

Of me desperately trying to hold onto you

As you kept slipping out of my hands

Out of my tight frightened hold.

And as dreaded nightmares

That shouldn't come true

What happened and how

I will never get over

Each millisecond was too long to count

I remember each word

The doctor and nurses

And all their expressions

Like a stab in the chest

The night too damning and far too dark

I wanted to hold you tight

And say to hell with this world.

The irony that left me broken

And guilt-ridden

Was that they had oxygen for me

When your lungs weren't formed,

That, they looked and searched

For a pulse in me

When it must have been reaching out to you,

That I was given chest compressions

While you lay cold upon a steel tray,

That when they sighed with relief

That I did breathe,

You had already entered eternity.

Morning brought in family and friends

Who lied to me at the doctor's instructions

That you were safe in an incubator,

So I prayed for you

But somehow I knew my prayers were unanswered

They were touching the ceiling and falling back in my lap,

So I began to question anyone who came near

Until with a sedative, the doctor threatened me

Her intentions were good but I needed answers

Should I pray or should I stop?

I bless the elderly nurse who was wise enough

To tell them that the lies should stop.

And as they approached my bedside

They didn't have to say a thing

For I found myself asking the unaskable,

"He's gone na?"

As I felt this flood of burning tears

Sting my eyes and sink my heart

I also felt you were at peace

Safe in the arms of Jesus

Safer than you'd have been in mine.

I knew now why my prayers had fallen flat

That you were beyond the need of them.

For you had risen to that peaceful realm

Beyond the grasp of earthly pain.

Now as they prepared your funeral

I saw a tiny little white coffin,

And you wrapped in soft cotton wool

Were laid in my arms to hold

And as I held you for that one single moment

I held a lifetime in that one single moment,

For I knew that's all I would ever have,

To gaze upon my baby boy

To soak in every detail of you

Your sweet face, jet-black hair

And tiny hands which were exactly like mine,

Was that one single moment!

And as I cradled you in my arms

They gathered around my hospital bed

To sing, 'I Surrender All',

The only verse that I could think of

Was Philippians 4:4,

I was to rejoice in Him always.

I thanked The Lord for you

For all the time I had with you

His to give and His to take.

Then after the last time

That my lips kissed your forehead

They left to bury your tiny body forever.

You brought such joy,

And yet left such sorrow!

You were supposed to be close,

Yet you're a chasm afar!

You were made for my arms

 Yet you left them empty…

You were to be mine forever

Yet you left me for an eternity …

You brought such hope,

but you left such despair.

A part of me died with you

Yet something new was born too,

A me who'd search beyond the blue

Trying to find meaning in your death

The reason why I still had breath.

You left me trying to peep

Behind death's heavy curtain…

If I could just catch a glimpse of you…

Oh, my child …

My little child!

They said there's always hope,

And that time is a great healer.

I said I seriously doubted them then,

And I still don't believe it now,

At least not in this story.

For this hole in my heart is still empty,

And as time goes on,

I'll never know what I've missed.

Would you have started shaving?

And would your voice have cracked?

And what would you have sounded like

When you'd call out to me, "Mummy."?

****

20. Forever In Your Corner

{To my second born, my beautiful daughter, Grace. This is my second poem to her. The first I shan't dare to add here for fear of her either disowning me or granting me that all too familiar eye-roll.

Daughters are special and this journey of motherhood has been most rewarding. It has been a fantastic fun filled experience where I have learnt more from her than she from me. I love her and have forced myself to consciously learn that she isn't an extension of me but her very own individual self. A capable and self-sufficient individual, who doesn't need me to gate-crash her decision making process or to be solution-finder for every crisis in her life. All she needs is the assurance that when she calls out to me, I will be there.}

It has been a privilege

To be a steward unto you,

To witness you grow

Into the person that you are,

To watch in awe

As you spread your wings to fly,

To stand forever in your corner

Rooting for you is a joy.

Yet, I try not to stand too close

But, I know, too far I cannot be

Because in this ring called life

Bouts are fought individually,

Just know that when the bell rings

And it is time to rest

I'll be there in your corner

With a towel and iced water.

Yes, I helped you learn how to walk

Looked out for you when you ran

But just because I'm your mother

Doesn't give me the right

For your dreams to smother.

You must walk your own path

Carve your own way

Cut through the lawn, if you may.

We may not see eye to eye

And that is just fine

We may believe differently

And even that's divine

Just because I've given you birth

It certainly isn't mandatory

That you need my seal of approval

To know your value and your worth.

You are your own person

And you are sensible

I don't need to be around

To know that you'll be fine,

You don't need to be perfect

But I know you'll be true

To yourself and your cause.

My darling, I trust you.

****

21. <u>Arise Oh Humanity! Arise!</u>

{We as adults in a society have lost the very milk of human kindness. We use our children to meet our own selfish needs ... mostly to boost our petty egos. Let's for a change, begin treating children as individual human entities. Let's give them the chance and the tools to equip them to live enriched lives.}

Arise oh humanity, Arise!

Arise for thy hour is here!

Let not time pass us by,

Let not our little children cry!

The future of our kind is in their little hands,

Let's guide tomorrow's rulers of our precious lands!

How dare we abuse the innocent child?

Are we really wicked or just out of our minds?

When education should be as free as air,

It's paisa - it's paisa that consumes all our care!

When their lives should be just of playing and learning,
Why are they stuck in a factory working?

When children should be just a bundle of joy,
We knot ourselves between a girl and a boy!

When her safest home should be her mother's womb,
How dare we transform it into a bloody tomb?

It's time to stop and re-evaluate our goal!
To renew our minds - To examine our soul!

If we ever want to be healed and whole,
We need to love and value our very own!

****

22. **Hate**

{Why do we hate someone because he's of a different religion or has a different opinion about a certain subject? Why do we categorise our fellow human beings in order to debase their existence with the sole purpose of satisfying the vilest form of self-righteousness?}

If the reason that you hate,

Is because one is of a different hue.

It's time to pause and introspect,

Your hateful point of view.

Coz hate has no boundaries,

It will eventually turn on you.

And in its rabid, morbid flames,

It recognises not, who's who!

For history stands to testify,

There is no glory in breeding hate.

That the bearer of the burden of hate,

Becomes the object of what he did generate!

So it's crucial to put a stop to the hate,
Before it ricochets off, and back on you!

For the only thing, hate can successfully do,
Is to bid humanity a gory adieu!

****

23. What's Your Threshold?

{The lack of empathy and the mental roadblocks which cause us to justify cruelty being meted out to a vulnerable set of people is horrendous. This can be well observed in so many different shades, ranging from domestic violence in the neighbour's house to genocides around the world. The victim blaming is appalling, to say the least.

But the question here is when do we decide that we are humane enough to take a stand against this injustice? Do we possess the soul to search for the courage to stand beside the oppressed? How often are we going to continue to turn a blind eye to the uncomfortable so that we avoid the disruption of our own comfort zone?}

What's your threshold mentally

When you see your neighbour hurt physically?

Does he bleed a different shade of red?

One that you don't recognise as a friend?

What makes you blind to his tears

Watch in silence as people laugh at his fears?

Are those threats for him alone?
Do you think they'll never boomerang home?

What's the threshold holding you back
When your neighbour is under attack?

Didn't you play cricket together?
Wasn't he just like your brother?

Who built your threshold ever so high?
That you fear to step over, lest you die?

Where is the spine that you lack?
Each time your brother is under attack?

Who built your threshold ever so high?
That you can watch him die without a sigh?

So what's the threshold holding you back
From helping a brother who's under attack?

Your brother is in pain

And you know he is in pain

You hear him cry

You watch his children die

You see his tears

You know his fears

The terror he lives in is not new

But it fails to strike a chord in you!

****

24. <u>Handsome!</u>

{In a world so focused on the exterior, we need to look beneath the layers and beyond the obvious to actually seek genuine souls. We need to filter 'the filters'!}

Handsome is what handsome does!

Let's test this proverb and see if it's true,

Coz the superficial will fade and jade,

So let's give value to where it's due.

He may just stop a zillion hearts,

He may be stylish and debonair,

But please open your eyes and walk away,

If all he does is blow hot air!

He may be the life of the party,

But if his jokes are mean and paltry,

Always at the expense of a soft target,

Understand, there is no humour in cruelty!

If for the downtrodden he takes no stand,
And for the voiceless, he refuses to speak,
No matter how puffed his biceps may be,
He is spineless, feeble, selfish, and weak!

If he is mean to animals and pets,
Thinks they're just a waste of money 'n time,
The man has not a loving heart,
And certainly isn't worth a dime!

If he holds his subordinates' ransom to wage,
A poor man's woes are insignificant,
No matter how dapper his three-piece suit,
Walk away from this obnoxious sycophant!

If he banks upon his parent's will,
And expects they'll always foot the bill,
Don't waste a moment on this lazy lump,
'Coz he won't work til he's cold and still!

No matter how wonderful when sober he is
But, if to the bottle his allegiance lies,
Until he decides to change his life,
It'll make no difference if you say goodbye!

If for his parents he, does not care,
And unto them is rude and odious,
Let his trophies shimmer on the shelf,
The man is a menace, his family's anguish!

Now, if any or all of the above is true,
Expect him to behave no differently to you,
For no matter how solemn that precious 'I do'
Unto his base nature, he will be true!

So Yes, handsome is as handsome does!
Handsome in thought and handsome in deed,
Someone who takes time to love and care,
Is someone who is truly handsome indeed!

****

25. His Lies

{A narcissist will lie through his teeth to you. He may be convincing in the beginning but as time goes on, you'll subconsciously find a particular pattern in all his verbal distortion. This will eventually become a guide map to navigate through all his tales and fibbery.

Don't let that get you down because that is who he is. You're not to blame and neither are you meant to be the saviour. All I can say is don't waste your time. Get up and leave with lessons learnt.}

If his lies flow easily

As if it is his mastery.

They will at times make no sense

Blaming you for every offence.

You'll find that he can lie at will

All for a petty 'n cheap thrill.

For some wayward entertainment

That'll question the essence of discernment.

So it's best to turn your eyes away

To see through the lies, then look away!

For why must you waste your life,

Over someone who's not worth the strife.

Just leave the liar on his own

Let him reap what he has sown.

Lest he cause you sleepless nights

Or drive you to the brink of suicide.

Burn the bridge, if there was one

As for the river, there was none.

For it was all just verbal garbage

Him conniving a mere mirage!

****

26. Oh, Pride!

{Pride… the downfall of many. It would be comical if it wasn't so exasperating}

Knowing that Pride is inversely proportionate

To the size of your brain,

Thinking about anyone other than self,

Must be a strain!

That's why you flap your words,

To praise yourself so much,

For the power to reason

Is frightfully double-dutch!

And as you laud yourself

On the pinnacle of imaginary illusion,

I hope your descent into reality,

Is a bone-breaking conclusion!

****

27. **Simple things**

{The early morning sun, a gentle breeze, the birds chirping, the dew-covered grass, a playful kitten and hyperactive pup.... May these treasures be yours forever!}

Simple things that bring you joy,

Simple things that make you smile,

You don't need a diamond ring,

Nor a ticket to a foreign floor.

All you need is a little peace,

And a reason for your heart to sing.

Simple things are far more precious,

Simple things endureth more,

You don't need all that glitter,

For even gold melts in the fire,

All you need is a little sunshine,

And the calm when life's a flitter!

Simple things may seem simple now,

But there'll come a time when you'll see,

The smile and joy they brought you once,

Will be the sunshine in which you'll bask,

For when the present becomes the past,

They'll be the only treasure that will last.

****

28. <u>Our Journeys</u>

{Sometimes we meet people along life's path who invariably walk beside us for a while. They may be friends, co-workers or even fellow passengers on a train. Those moments shared and those stories exchanged are always enriching. Those ideas help you see life from a different point of view. I've made some dear friends on buses and trains who have influenced my life.

When I was around 13 years old I met a newly married couple on a train bound for Mumbai (then called Bombay). The lady told me about how wonderful NCC was... sure enough a couple of years later I was marching proudly in my rice-water-starched uniform, piloting the chief guest and the school principal to hoist our national flag on the 15th of August. (It was raining heavily but that's a different story.) Just a brief encounter with a lady who has absolutely no clue that the impact of her words has gifted me a lifetime of beautiful memories...to her and countless others... Thank you!

Decades later, I was travelling from Devali to Delhi by train when I was asked to teach grammar to members of a State Jr. Chess Team. Teaching these young teenagers on the train gave me such joy as it felt like Deja Vu or rather one of life's full circles taking place. After the grammar lesson was over, they decided to repay me by teaching me chess...which concluded with them roasting each other till the end of the journey.

*These short encounters create such precious memories
which are etched in my heart forever.}*

Upon that journey short and sweet,

Meeting you was a divine treat!

Thank you for being there,

For all the time that you did spare!

Like little fairies from the mist,

Sprinkling gold dust to change the gist!

Thank you for being the catalyst,

Sharing your experiences without resist!

For highlighting a different avenue,

Something that was completely new!

In those hours of travelling interstate,

Into one family we did amalgamate.

So thank you from the depth of my heart,

For life's journey of which you were a part!

****

29. __Time__

{Let's not waste it.}

Time!

You never really were mine!

Time!

A falsehood of eternity sublime!

Time!

A fleeting gift ever so divine!

Time!

For we know not when we'll cross that line!

Time!

Wrapped in the pseudo-security of a pretty chime!

Time!

You never really were mine!

Time!

Oh time!

****

30. **Money**

"The love of money is the root of all evil,"
Says the Holy Book!

For money can buy things,

That money shouldn't buy!

For love, respect, and dignity,

Were never meant to be sold!

But avarice stems from a heart,

That will worship with a lie!

For money is a blindfold,

Of the finest quality!

And when it lines the pockets,

It shrouds the fiend for friend!

And in this false illusion,

With deceptions running high!

Words do drip with honey,

With backstabbing in the end!

So in a world that chases money,

Look for things it cannot buy!

Like those who will stand by you,

Though your pockets be high and dry!

Seek for Love Respect and Dignity,

Whose value is truly high!

For that's the priceless treasure,

Which money is too poor to buy!

****

31. <u>Hospital Truths</u>

{It's when times are bad that you get to know your real friends.}

As I lay my head down,

Upon this unfamiliar pillow,

In a cold hospital bed,

And as the lights,

Are turned down low,

My friends and well-wishers,

I got to know!

Those who took,

The time to call,

Those who texted,

Back and forth,

Those who cared,

The evidence showed,

And those that didn't,

Was evident too!

For my heart.

Already knew.

There were actually

No surprises.

Just that I hoped,

That what I knew,

Would be somehow,

A tad untrue,

But it isn't,

Alas, it isn't!

****

32. The Spiritual Camouflage

{Some of the most dangerous masks are the spiritual ones. They are used to manipulate even the most learned and educated. It's so very crucial to identify this well-constructed camouflage, for it is wrapped in all the righteous phrases and some cunningly crafted deeds.}

When you want to fulfil your evil little task

Why in God's name must you really bask?

Just to complete your personal agenda

You've used God's name for selfish propaganda.

That somehow you've climbed that spiritual rung

Where instead of Him, your praises be sung.

You've made Him into some mystic deity

Who's appointed you as His earthling entity.

Stop using His name

To garner your fame.

For you stand upon a feigned pedestal
And its crumble to destruction is, but inevitable.

So stop spinning your theory of a heavenly mirage

For can see right through your spiritual camouflage.

****

33. Resuscitate The Decaying Soul

*{'Every action has an equal and opposite reaction'...
Newton was almost poetic and definitely philosophical
with this law. What most people don't realise is that life
comes full circle! There is no way we can escape the
consequences of our actions.}*

When deceit through lies and shelved truths

From an internal maelstrom is your goal

You deceive no other for very long

But your own decaying soul.

For deceit becomes an insalubrious custom

That inevitably deceives the very deceiver

Who so entwined in frivolous deception

Perceives not himself as the final receiver.

So resuscitate your decaying soul

Or be the fruit of what you've sown

Stop the lies, unshelve the truth

Prove to yourself as a human you've grown

****

34. Life's Race

{It is one thing to be nostalgic and it is completely another thing to be morbid and revengeful. While reminiscing about the past almost always brings us comfort, we have to be very careful that we don't get stuck in the quicksand of bitterness and what-ifs. It's a place no healthy soul wants to be stuck in. Accepting the past and moving on is the only healthy way to continue life's journey. After all, even the present is tick-tocking its way quickly into the future.}

Looking back over my shoulder

As I run life's race

Keeps me faltering in my track

And losing time and pace.

Caught in the web of yesterday's threads

They have their claws in my today

Blindfolding me to my tomorrow

Distorting the beauty of today.

It's time to now pull down those webs
Break those claws and those threads
Take a deep breath and open your eyes
To focus on today and look ahead.

For yesterday may have built today
But it doesn't mean you have to stay
For yesterday's gone and today's at hand
And tomorrow is just a step away.

So go run your race and don't look back
Winners never do!
Go, run into that early morn'
And build a brand new dawn.

****

35. I'm Sorry

{How we have failed Jesus!!! In every way possible. The scriptures have been made so complex with everything blown out of proportion. We have begun to focus on the frills. A far flung image from what it was meant to be. Tragic that the yeast of the pharisees has indeed spread!}

From the crib to the cross!

From the star to the thunder!

From the shepherds to The Shepherd!

Your life was to suffer!

To stop a woman being stoned!

To call an untouchable your daughter!

To make sure no poor ate alone!

To hold the hand of a leper!

You stood for the truth!

So you were killed with a lie!

A rebel you were labelled!

Who was fit but to die!

But you rose three days later!

For the truth can't be buried!

You hope to show me the way!

To go where love is needed!

Today we celebrate your birth!

We celebrate your resurrection!

But do we celebrate your walk?

Your courage, Your conviction?

Do we walk with the poor?

Are we the voice of the voiceless?

Do we stand for the oppressed?

Are we the defender of the defenceless?

I'm sorry we've failed you,

With zest misconstrued!

I'm sorry we've failed you,

For all that your life stood!

****

36. Be Your Own Break Of Day!

{A fairy tale princess waiting for her knight in shining armour is a myth. You are strong enough to rescue yourself. You go, girl!}

When all your world is in darkness
And the darkness envelops you
And you cannot comprehend
What lies two feet in front of you
The path to take is unfathomable
For the path you cannot see
And that darkness all around you
Seems like an eternity.

Now, ideally, when the time is right
You may see a golden glimmer,
Miles away in the distance
Where the land should meet the sky,
You may see the break of dawn
Which may transform the entire view
And your eyes may witness the horizon
Where you may gaze at many a hue.

But what if this dawn is eclipsed
And isn't happening for you...
Will you wait and will you sob?
Allow this darkness to continue?
And will you allow the world to litigate,
Of what becomes your fate?
Or will you look into yourself?
And be the dawn unto you?

Will you be your own glimmer?
Be it gold or be it grey?
And will you draw your own horizon,
Where the you meets you?
Will you light your own path?
And carve your own way?
So will you be your own dawn?
Your own break of day?

And once you seek, you will find
There's so much light within you
With innate strength to ensure
That your horizon has hues galore.
That you may choose your path to be
For your light will set you free.
So go be your very own dawn!
And be the break of every morn'!

****

37. **Me**

{Do you know how valuable you are? You are you, and there is only one you... That sounds cliché ... yes, of course, because it's true. Ask your kids or the pets you feed. You as a person are irreplaceable.}

When I fell in love with me
I stopped longing for you,
When I fell in love with me
I got what I was due.

When I fell in love with me
Life fell into place,
When I fell in love with me
I found new worth and grace.

When I fell in love with me
I discovered what I was worth,
When I fell in love with me
I knew no lack or dearth.

The fact that I am me
And there is only one me,
There is value I now see
Because I fell in love with me.

****

38. <u>Imagination</u>

{In the hope of conceiving the tangible through the haze of the intangible we need to gaze through the kaleidoscope of our imagination to bring forth a better reality.}

What allows us to dream,
A dream that hasn't hit reality yet?

What fuels us to hope,
A hope that hasn't brought peace yet?

What gives us the courage to fight,
A fight that hasn't been won yet?

What gives us the peace to rest,
A rest that hasn't been perceived yet?

Our Imagination.

Thus let our imagination dream
A dream that fuels our hope
A hope that gives us courage
The courage to fight for peace
The peace that allows us to rest.

****

39. Just Be The Friend She'd Call

{What a blessing it is to be that friend in deed}

She's on the floor
And can think no more
She's just been to hell and back
Her lip is bleeding from that stinging whack.
Just be the friend she'd call.

She's standing in front of that closed door
Discovering that she's welcome there no more
A lifetime of memories snatched away
Her world's come crashing down in a day.
Just be the friend she'd call.

Her trust in him is evaporating
The pedestal she placed him on is disintegrating,
Discovering the life, she's living is all a lie
That he doesn't care if all night she'd cry.
Just be the friend she'd call.

Just be the friend she'd call
The one that won't make her feel small.
The one who'll be her sounding board
Who'll also make sure she's seen and heard
Who'll hear her through the heartbreak
And support her through the remake.
The strength to fight is all within her
She just needs your help to gather it Dear.
All she needs is moral support
That which only a friend can bring forth.

Just be the friend she'd call
The one she can count on through it all.
The one she knows will help her stand tall
Just be that friend she'd call.

****

40. The Dawning

{May you heal.}

Who are you?
And what are you worth?

Have you been rejected?
Have you been called dirt?

Been called a burden?
A cross to carry?

Felt like a misfit?
Asked to leave and not tarry?

A curse to the womb?
The cause of a tomb?

Did all these adjectives
Take seed in your heart?

Did they seem true
As they grew in you?

So you acted out
To the hurt that you felt.
Justifying to the sayer
That they were rightly said.

They all saw the fruit
In your angry eyes
But they heard not the seed
In your silent cries.

So who are you?
Do you truly know?
Deep inside
What makes you, you?

Then that's all that matters
For the journey to begin
The realisation
Of what's hidden within.

 It's time you sit back
Close your eyes and be still.
To take a deep breath
And stay calm at will.

Jot down a list
And this is a must
If you want to heal
Then this is the crux.

For your eyes need to read
Who you truly are
And what was previously said
Is not true by far.

Uproot those words
From your heart and your head,
All those words
Which were negatively said.

They are not your adjectives
They never ever were
They were just toxins
Somebody else's burdens.

That they were just words
From an unhealed heart
Hurt breeding hurt
Right from the start.

And as you realise
Who you truly are
Imperfectly perfect
What a treasure you are!

May this be the beginning
Of healing the hurting
To start a new journey
In the light of this dawning…

****

About The Author

Eleanor is an Indian teacher and writer, who writes to awaken women. Awakening them to begin to value themselves for what they are truly worth!
With a Master's Degree in English Literature and a Post Graduate Diploma in Human Rights, she has sought to bring the two together in this book of poetry.
Using her life experiences she encourages women all around the world to step out of the shadows, walk into the sunlight and never look back.

Her advice to all women of all ages is - *"Girl, you're not alone. Look around you and find another sister to lift up and in lifting her, you rise too."*

The message that this book gives is that the dark times are seasonal and that the dawn has to break at some point or the other but the brilliance of the light depends upon you.

****